For Louise Freymann and Jeffrey Freymann-Weyr,
whom I have loved since we were pups. — S.F.

Copyright © 2002 by Play With Your Food, LLC
All rights reserved. Published by Scholastic Press, a division of Scholastic Inc.,
Publishers since 1920. SCHOLASTIC, SCHOLASTIC PRESS and the LANTERN LOGO
are trademarks and/or registered trademarks of Scholastic Inc.

Book design by Elizabeth B. Parisi
Photography by Nimkin/Parrinello

Library of Congress data available

ISBN 0-439-11016-5

10 9 8 7 6 5 4 3 2   02 03 04 05 06
Printed in Mexico   49
First edition, September 2002

DOG FOOD

Written and Illustrated by Saxton Freymann

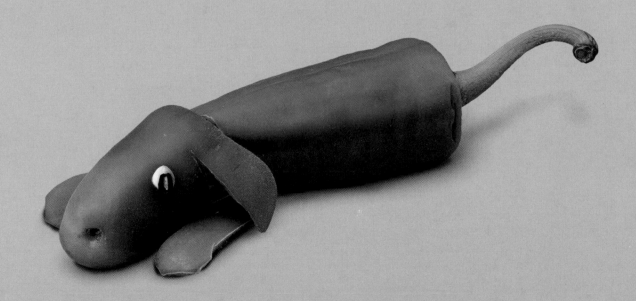

ARTHUR A. LEVINE BOOKS

An Imprint of Scholastic Press / New York

Good dog!

Bad dog

Mad dog

(In the doghouse)

Hot dog

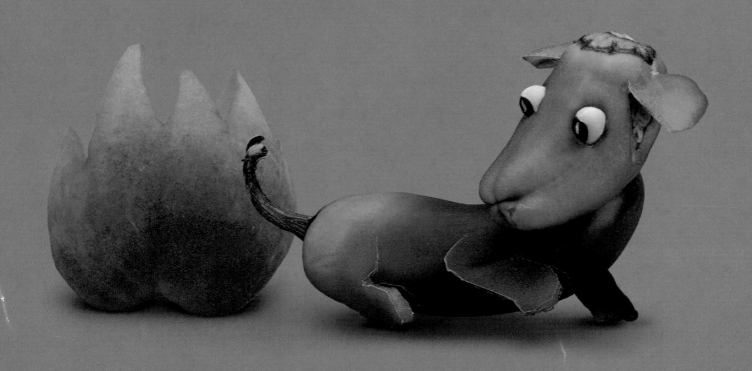

Chilly dog

Top dog

Underdog

Dog paddle

Dog bowl

Dog catcher

Dog tag

Dog show

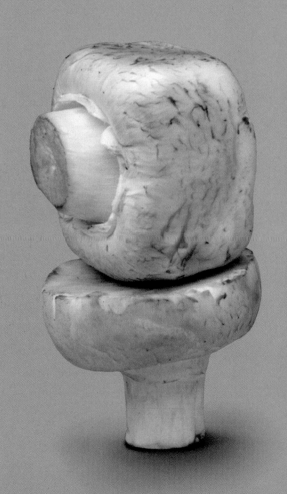

FIGHT

Dog eat Dog

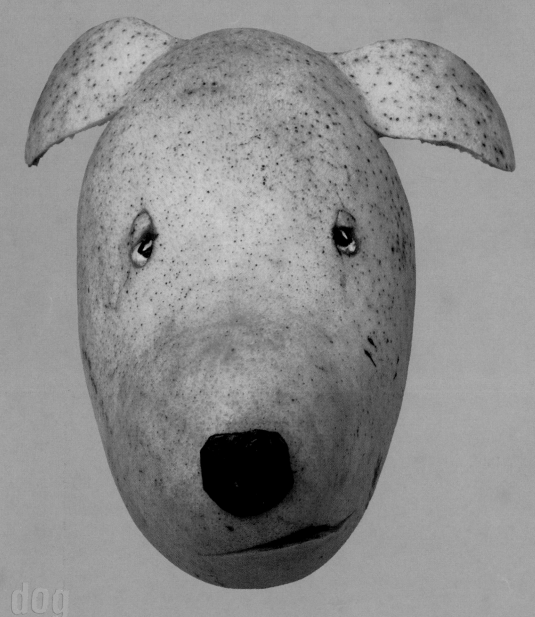

Sick

as a dog

Sick puppy

Doggy bag

Pup tent

Lucky dog

Puppy love

Working
like a dog

Dog whistle

Dog pound

(Dog wood)

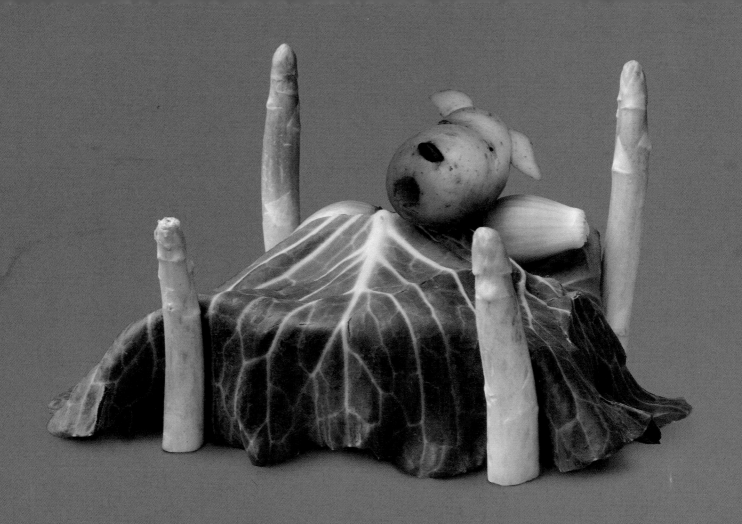

Dog tired

Shhh...Let sleeping dogs lie.

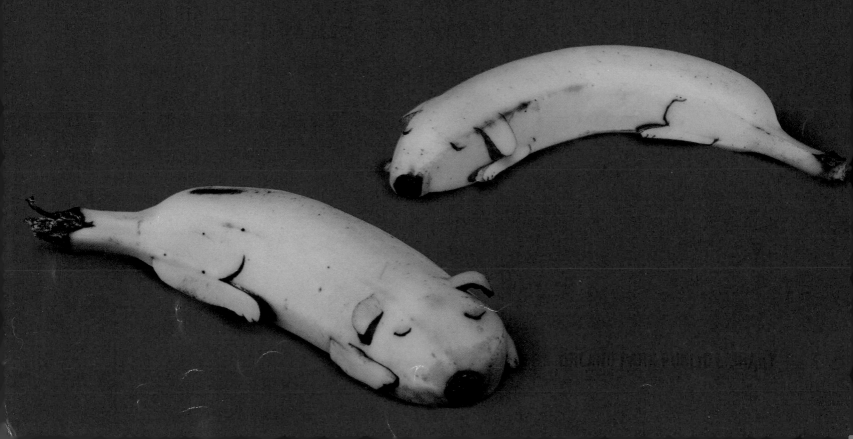